Butterfliology.

butter·fli·ology

—— SECOND EDITION ——

*The art of defining yourself for yourself
Free thought*

J. Azules Amor

Butterfliology.

butter·fli·ology

— SECOND EDITION —

butter·fli·ology
(noun)
free thought, defining yourself for yourself,
embracing and loving your whole self

Copyright © 2023 by J. Azules Amor

All rights reserved. No part of this publication may be reproduced, distributed, or transmitted in any form or by any means, including photocopying, recording, or other electronic or mechanical methods, without the prior written permission of the publisher, except in the case of brief quotations embodied in critical reviews and certain other noncommercial uses permitted by copyright law. For permission requests, write to the publisher, addressed "Attention: Permissions Coordinator," at the address below.

J. Azules Amor LLC, Publishing
500 N. Washington Street Unit 1131
Rockville, Maryland 20850 and/or jamor.azules@gmail.com

Ordering Information:
Quantity sales. Special discounts are available on quantity purchases by corporations, associations, and others. For details, contact the publisher at the address above. Orders by U.S. trade bookstores and wholesalers. Please send requests to: jamor.azules@gmail.com

Printed in the United States of America
ISBN 978-1-7358804-95
Second Edition Print 2023

Front Cover Image illustrated by: Kozakura
Interior Book Design by: Kozakura @ fiverr.com
Johari's Window creators: Joseph Luft and Harrington Ingham in 1955

Dedicated to Ruth "Late" Moon Brown, grandmother extraordinaire, and my three breaths of life, Kawand, Khairi, Khisan.

Onward and upward for the lion and the butterfly. My heart rests easy with you

butter.fli.ology

Foreward xiii
Introduction 1
Love 9
Divinity, You Are My Focus 15
Orgasms 19
Self Preservation 23
First Mind 27
BEware Of Spiritual Vampires 31
Cocooning 35
Universe, Teach Me 39
Metamorphosis 43
The Lay Of The Land 47
Energy Is Everything 53
Mentorship 57
Don't Activate My Crazy 61
Butterfli Journey/Self Discovery 65
Spirituality 71

Foreward

In preparation for the re release and second anniversary of 'Butterfliology: Free Thought; The Art of Defining Yourself for Yourself, has come with some new thoughts on if and what needs to be changed within this Second Edition. I can tell you that, this book and the knowledge within is for a specific group of free thinkers. Those that are free spirited enough to want to embrace change and a new mindset. The Truth is everything is not for everybody, and when we try to make it so, we lose the essence of who we really are and instead fall into the very trap of allowing others to define the perimeters of our comfortability.

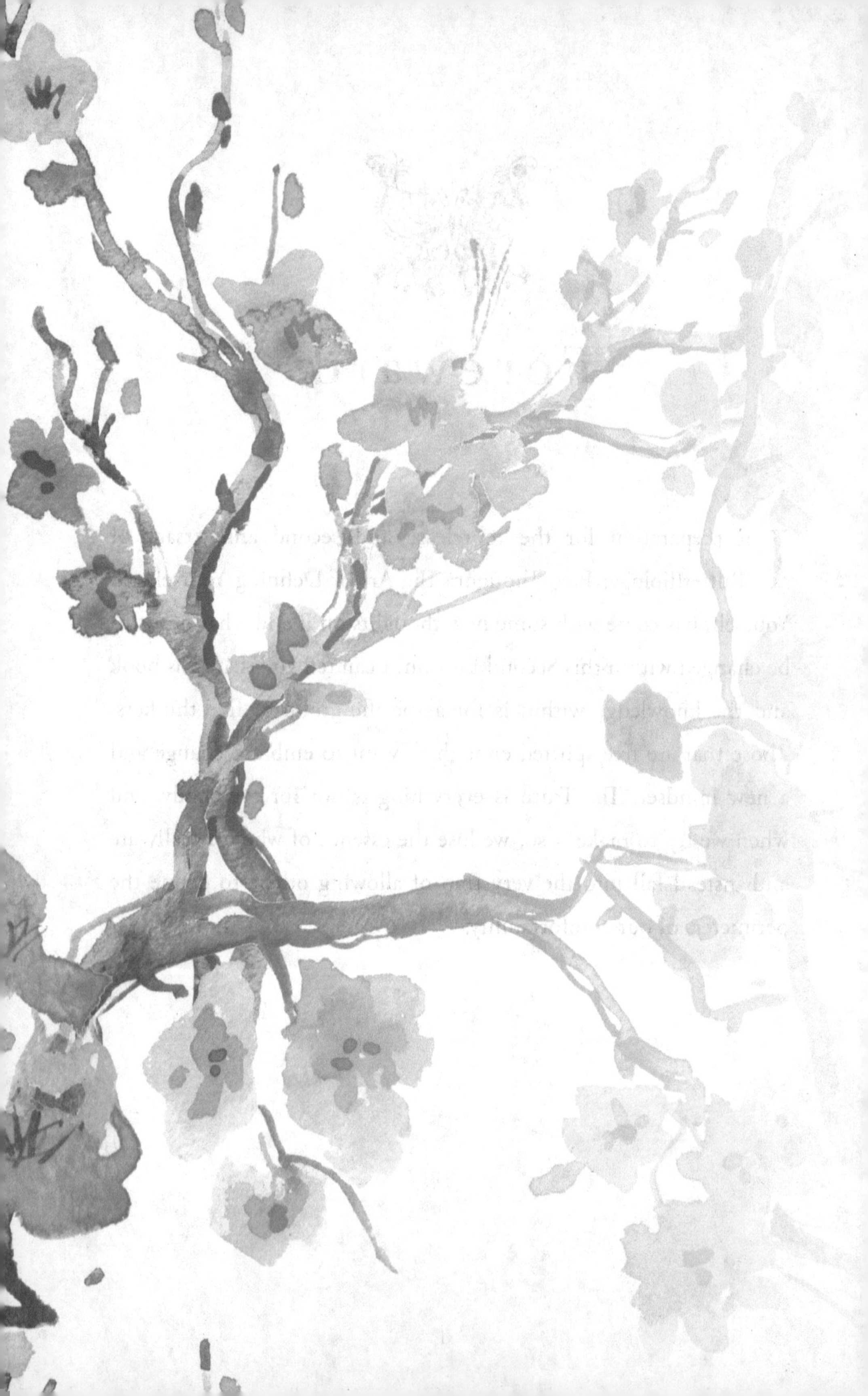

Introduction

This project is a long time coming. It represents a journey, a metamorphosis of sorts, that speaks directly from my soul. I believe, with every fiber of my being, that it is premised on a universal concept in which others can relate, and it does so on so many levels. It is thought provoking, renders deep thought, and in some instances, recalibration of both thoughts and self. It is also a combination of life lessons, experiences, and lessons from The Universe. Many times, we refrain from following The Divine entity within ourselves and allow other people's voices, fears, and lack of spiritual connection to self to manifest our fears and swallow our dreams whole. We then, refrain from dreaming and live and wallow in self doubt, never realizing our greatest potential.

The Rebels

I know that I am different. I always have been, and that's okay. I always have been, and that's okay. What has encouraged me through the years that there are others that are different also and propelled me to be myself and embrace all that makes me who I am. Some of those pioneers are Oprah Winfrey, Erykah Badu, Jill Scott, Prince, Spike Lee, Celia Cruz, Iyanla Vanzant, Taraji P. Henson, Regina Hall, women I have grown up seeing in my community, church ladies, co workers that became friends, family members, Tyler Perry, Lena Waithe, Diana Ross, Millie Jackson, Chaka Khan, Cyndi Lauper, Boy George. and countless others that have influenced me to continue to 'think outside the box' and embrace who I am. And, I encourage you to do the same. I encourage you to bow to no one's thoughts or fancy, to believe in yourself, no matter what the circumstances. The people I mentioned in the above commentary gave no concern about the thoughts and opinions of others and lived or live their lives accordingly. I implore you to surround yourself with positive energy and to reject and refrain from those that mean you harm and attempt to dissuade you from your greatness. I keep my circle tight, and through that I have unknowlingly created my tribe.

A Turning Moment

Reading 'The Secret' was life changing and life evolving for me. It was part of my journey. Since that first read, I have re read it several times and refer to it in my mindset and practice, although I sometimes forget to follow what I have learned and that self doubt will creep in and rear its ugly head. I am forever grateful to Chef Skai for introducing me to that diamond, crystal knowledge.

YOLO

We only have one life to live, that we remember. In other words, if we do live more than one life, we only remember that one. Therefore, it is up to us to live that life to the fullest, mistakes, victories, and all. All of our experiences are the sum of who we are. That, to me, is one of the most challenging aspects to finally embrace, because people try to make us feel ashamed of our mistakes, our f* ups. In the same breath, they tell us that everyone makes mistakes, while not providing us the room to make our own.

I have learned that you can learn something from all ages and all walks of life. Some of the greatest thinkers and analyzers I know are my sons. Young people that I have mentored have also provided me with some of the greatest perspectives. And sitting on the porch with some of the elders in the community, talking with them gave me some of my greatest insight that has steered my life.

Beautiful Story

The story behind the song by Crystal Waters, is a fabulous example and blueprint for the very concept. Her song, Gypsy Woman which years later, I found was actually inspired by a homeless woman that she met. It's a beautiful story that is inspiring and serves as a thought provoking moment.

So often we will talk ourselves out of a thought or idea because we believe that it's too strange or no one will understand it. We fear rejection, and that fear can and sometimes paralyzes us into not being our true selves, and we must, above all else, be true to who and what we really are. The Universe has designed us that way and it is up to us to preserve, persevere, and to self advocate for that which is within us.

Future Vision

And I want it to become the norm instead of the exception in this country and all over the world, but specifically in this country, because we have not caught up with the rest of the world when, as it pertains to this...I want it to become the norm instead of the exception that people are accustomed to a Black Girl speaking Spanish, or German, or Russian, or Mandarin, or a variance of other languages other than English. Why is she mentioning that, you may ask? Well, we as a people, have been unknowingly been programmed to limit ourselves and our abilities. We do not take the time to learn multiple things or enhance multiple talents, gifts, or skills because society has trained us to doubt, underestimate ourselves, under utilize our talents, think in the one income mindset, and to focus on only one skill at a time. I am a Black Gyurl, Black woman who speaks Spanish as a second language and that needs to be the norm and not the exception. We need to start teaching it to our children early and presenting the attitude that all languages are their language. A language does not belong to one set of people or another...although some choose to believe as such. Part of being a butterfly is allowing yourself to be free. It is allowing your inner being to speak so loudly that it is heard over all the other thoughts in your head. BEing a butterfly is a mindset and eventually a lifestyle that you embrace along with your tribe.

butter.fli.ology

What is butterfliology? It is free thought. Embracing Spirituality. Thinking outside the box, being different, unique, and embracing it. Defining yourself for yourself and listening and being in tune with your inner spirit. It's embracing your natural talents, gifts, and abilities while simultaneously enhancing and perfecting those gifts, talents, and abilities. It's accepting your strengths, weaknesses, flaws, and embracing and loving your whole self. It's putting you first...and by doing it shows others what you want and how to deservingly treat you. butterfliology is freedom and soul thought.

BE magnificent
BE adventurous
BE courageous
BE considerate
BE happy
BE diligent
BE original
BE loyal
BE dramatic
BE incredible
BE amazing
BE outstanding
BE valiant
BE creative

BE confident
BE empowered
BE fabulous
BE inquisitive
BE kind
BE determined
BE fearless
BE powerful
BE more
BE majestic
BE imaginative
BE understanding
BE awesome
BE amazing

Butterfli Thought:

"The process of transformation is not about becoming something that we weren't. It's about unveiling what we were the whole time."

- (7.29.2018) William Paul Young

Butterfli Thought:

"You can't take everyone with you.
Sometimes, you have to leave them behind."

- J. Azules Amor

Love

*"Know your value. Know your worth.
So, you can formulate and establish your ground rules early."*

- J. Azules Amor

Ask for what you want, and be willing to walk away if you don't get it. I have learned to ask once. If the person does not fulfill the request wholeheartedly and with a willing an open heart, be willing to walk away. Be prepared to do so. Refrain from providing any person a blueprint of your love and heart. A probationary period is a must. It gives time for the representative to appear and leave.

Have I always followed this rule? There have been times when I have failed to do so, but that's from where my knowledge and understanding emerge. I absolutely do my best to do so though. There have been times that I have forgotten and gotten swept away in the connection, and had to recalibrate and get back on track. That's human. In those times, I have had to forgive myself and continue on my journey. When you know better, you do better. We have to allow ourselves these mistakes, even when we know better. Sometimes, we get swept up in emotion and forget the things we know because love is not based on logic. It is a powerful emotion. Powerful. It is through the knowledge of these things, we learn from our mistakes, analyze and embrace what we know, as sound advice.

What I can tell you is that, if you do follow this knowledge, to the best of your ability, you have a better chance of avoiding what I discuss in my chapter, "Don't Activate My Crazy." This chapter, this zone, is the one I try to stay in but sometimes that alter ego appears and...we try to keep her calm, happy, satisfied. In the meantime, let's keep the focus on this "Love" chapter.

If you are coming out of a relationship, and you no longer know what you want or are looking for in another person, potential mate, it's okay to take the time to be with one's self until you figure it out and heal. In that, you may not know what you want, but you know what you don't want. That's a start. Begin piecing together your new idea of your new mate. Consider someone out of the country or region where you grew up or where you reside. Be willing to be open to learn new languages and/or cultures to pursue your goal. Be willing to travel, or even consider living outside of the country. Your potential mate could be on the other side of the world or the region waiting for you. Be limitless in your idea and pursuit for love.

Butterfli Journal Excerpt:

"The person has to believe they deserve you for the relationship to work. They must be aware of their self worth and proclaim its Truth. The lack of that key component can allow others to come in and cast doubt, potentially destroy and deteriorate what is currently and has been built. A strong foundation of love and self acceptance must be present and manifests itself boldly. Refrain from emotional purgatory. Give of yourself what you can. Refrain from giving to the point of depletion. Depletion leads to resentment. Be comfortable with setting boundaries for both your personal and emotional space"

- J. Azules Amor

Butterfli Thought:

"People that have never been able to live out their dreams, will never believe in yours."

- J. Azules Amor

"Divinity, You Are My Focus."

- J. Azules Amor

Be willing to let old friendships, relationships, familyships go. We are beings of constant change and evolution. That means nothing stays the same, and that we and everything is in a constant state of change. Nothing is static. Why should that change for the sake of a relationship, friendship, familyship, partnership, if it no longer works for you? Friendships, or any relationship can be seasonal, and some friendships, for example are meant to last a lifetime. Others are seasonal and their season may be one day, ten years, thirty years, and the season ends. If the relationship no longer fits who you are or matches your evolutionary process, be willing to let that go. Too many times, we keep people around for habit or we have convinced ourselves that we are obligated to that kinship because it has always been that way and it is the way it is supposed to be. Be willing to protect your energy at all costs.

Butterfli thoughts:

Ask more questions. Know your worth. Self acceptance. Self love. Trust your instincts.

Orgasms

Orgasms are amazing gifts from God. They are a spiritual release formed in the physical, and are manifestations of our divine connection and space in the Universe. To deny oneself of this primal, powerful, and sophisticated, and necessity is to deny one the same needed components of breath, air, food, and water. It is indeed a necessary component of life.

Sometimes, we forget that in our busy lives we are not holding still to enjoy the peace, tranquility, and stillness of life. The euphoria that comes before, during, and after a climatic interlude is where delirium and combustion meet. As energy is everything. Hence, the reason your ends stand on end open and ready like millions of sea anemone, it's a beautiful thing. An orgasm is a beautiful call to the Universe and a reminder that Divinity exists.

The problem is when this powerful and beautiful gift is taken out of context of its purpose and intent and therefore used, abused, mutilated, humiliated, murdered, suffocated, degraded, and used with ill intent. When these things happen it tinges the beauty, serenity, and puritanical powers that are yielded to its substance. An orgasm is a spiritual experience in the form of a physical release. Guard it well. Protect it well. And just like any gift, it is to be treasured, and neither given or received lightly. It is your God given right to have and give one with yourself, and it is your choice to give and receive that pleasure with other consenting, of age beings. Orgasms are purveyors of the soul. They provide the benefits of cleansing and clearing your energy. You can think better, breathe better, sleep better, and improves overall function. Without orgasms comes blocked and stagnant energy that eventually leads to a barrage of health issues. Once again this is for consenting, of age, human beings which include the first principle, self pleasure.

Self Preservation

*"Sometimes, our light is brighter that we even realize.
Others recognize it before you do. Sometimes, people are drawn to
your energy because they are hungry."*

- J. Azules Amor

Self preservation is everything. It is the key to the wholeness of your soul. Within the concept of self preservation, individuals, especially women, mothers are made to feel guilty, inadequate, or labeled selfish if they practice self preservation.

It is the key to the wholeness of your soul. Within the concept of self preservation, individuals, especially women, mothers are made to feel guilty, inadequate, or labeled selfish if they practice self preservation.

Each person has to figure out what self preservation looks like for them. Some examples of what that looks like are turning off your phone, and shutting down from everyone and everything for a time period, not cooking if you don't feel like it or your heart is not into it. Allowing others, outside of your children, to figure out for themselves. Self preservation could look like getting off your chest how you feel even if the other person does not want to hear it.

Self preservation is your saying f* it to everyone and everything else at the time and putting yourself first. This does not include selfish acts such as affairs, or acts that would result in serious emotional, physical, or spiritual harm for others. That's not what butterflies do. It is in the definite terms, the art and practice of loving oneself, while embracing the belief and concept that you deserve to be happy, fulfilled, and whole.

"Butterfli Journal Excerpt from note to self:

"My goal is to take care of myself today. To work on my writing, which is my calling. To make or move appointments that will enhance my self care and my greater good. To begin the foundation of my charity work. To make arrangements with creditors that will propel me closer to my goals. To continually practice self care and self love and to strive for solid empowerment and independence from a job I no longer love and that does not love me back. To be bold in my choices and remember each day to live my Truth. I will be a great writer and I will be known as such, and now is the time to embrace that, to embrace that person and the core of who I really am. I deserve to be appreciated and my path and future shines brightly. I am thankful and grateful to God Almighty, Jehovah, Jah, Allah for my Blessings and purpose in life. I know that coincidence is an illusion and all steps are leading me to my path, my destiny. When we don't move ourselves and take heed, God will make us uncomfortable to change our circumstances and discourage stagnation..."

- J. Azules Amor

Make lists of what you need to do or what you need to accomplish. Feed your spirit constantly with good messages and wonderful energy.

Similar to Gabrielle Union's character on Being Mary Jane, I leave myself sticky notes or write notes of positive affirmations. Union's character was definitely on to something, with leaving the positive messages around her at her every turn, and embracing other's knowledge. She knew the benefits of surrounding yourself with positive energy and infusing and invoking that energy. We also observed how Mary Jane made sure her home was her sanctuary. That space became what she needed it to be. She exhibited the importance of that.

Butterfli Journal Excerpt:

"Sometimes, it's not about other people's feelings. It's about you. A friend may not understand why, at the time, you cannot give her any time or attention, why you're not available for her phone calls, or why you're simply not in the mood to listen to what she's experiencing or going through at the time. And that's perfectly okay. It's your job to be okay. It's not your job to be everyone's savior. It's not your job to bear everyone's cross just because you love them or they are important in your life. Sometimes, they just won't understand. And that's okay too. In those moments, they need to consult with their God or whatever other activities they need to do to carry through from their difficult moment. Once you get yourself situated, once you're able to take on someone else's sh* that's when you can give of yourself, but never to the point of depletion. If you feel your energy being drained from someone else's gravitational pull, it's time to pull yourself back from the situation or shutdown to preserve your energy. You must put you and your well being before others."

- J. Azules Amor

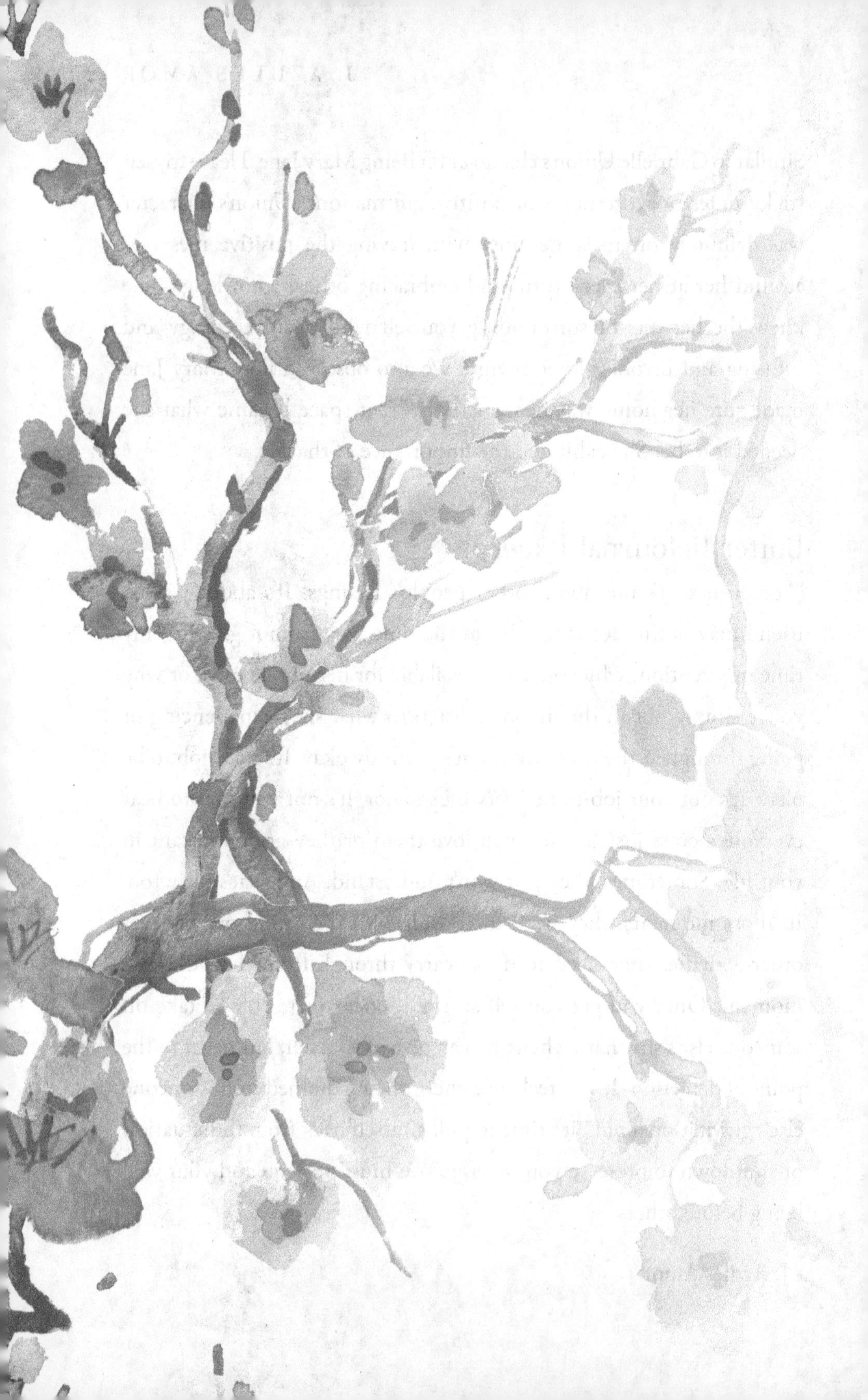

First Mind

Trust your instincts. Trust your vibes. And, follow your first mind. I know instantly if there is repulsive energy around me. I may not be able to explain it. I may not even fully recognize it at the time, but my spirit does. It recognizes the energy, the vibrations. Trust yourself. Be in tune with yourself. Energy is ever changing, but it is present in all things. All living or non living matter contains energy. Depending on how in tune you are with yourself, your energy, what you allow in your body, your space determines how quickly or accurately you respond to your energy and the energy around you.

We have all experienced either when we have or when we have negated to follow our first mind. For example, your instinct told you to choose a certain number, answer, or drive a certain direction, avoid a certain direction, or some other internal instruction that you either followed or did not follow. The outcome of that decision was a result of you either following or not following your first mind. You say, "I started to do that or I should have followed my first mind." The point is that this is something that in which we can all relate and we should refrain from discounting that powerful entity. It is an energy that leads us. I make practice of it when I get on elevators, for example. There was a time when, if there was a person on an elevator and I hesitated because I felt uncomfortable for a reason that I could not explain at the time, I no longer worry about it. I used to think that I did not want to be rude or appear rude and had more concern about that stranger's feelings than I had for my own safety and well being. When you respect and honor your first mind and put into daily practice, you are following your God given instincts. Some call it the Sixth Sense. In whatever name you want to call it, follow it. It is meant as a gift of protection.

BEware Of Spiritual Vampires

"People that have never been able to live out their dreams, will never believe in yours."

- J. Azules Amor

You cannot share your dreams or vision with everyone. Dream killers and stealers, also known as Spiritual Vampires do exist. They will, if allowed, suck the very life from your dreams and aspirations until there is nothing left. This is why you have to protect your energy. This is why you have to keep your circle tight. This is why you have to follow your instincts and your first mind. This is why you have to regenerate your energy through cocooning. This is why it is important to have your tribe.

If you will remember, in the chapter talking about love, I said, "Ask for what you want, and be willing to walk away if you don't get it." All of these actions and this mindset is important to stave away Spiritual Vampires. You've experienced them. We all have. Example, I told an ex boyfriend years ago, I wanted to write a book. His response was, if you give away all your secrets, someone will steal them from you and take credit. The result was I shelved my first book project. To this day, I have yet to publish it and it could have generated more money for my family as well as helped countless others. I shall publish that book, but the point is I told my dream to the wrong person, and instead of hope and optimism, he instilled fear. He, unknowing to himself, was being a Spiritual Vampire. I am sure knowing the good hearted person that he was, did not intend on doing so, but nevertheless, he did. He projected his fears or a personal experience from him onto me. The result was blocked blessings for myself and others that could have benefited from my knowledge and experience.

We want to share good news with others. Sometimes, we can but we have to be cautious in doing so because everyone does not necessarily mean us good or know how to dream. If you tell it to a person who does not embrace dreams and follow their spiritual path, they can drain your energy and your spirit faster than a hole in a sugar bag. You must be careful. Being careful is not synonymous with being fearful, but just know that everyone does not mean you any good. That's why it is imperative to have your tribe and your circle.

Spiritual Vampires are trapped by their own mind. How can they believe in your dreams when they lack the ability to believe in their own? They may not mean to be that negative source, but they are (that negative source) all the same. Spiritual Vampires can be in any form. They can be in the form of a mate, significant other, parent, family member, friend, or foe. Keep your circle tight and be mindful of the words you send into the Universe.

Cocooning

" I don't want to be bothered...and leave me the f* alone." We've all been there at one time or another. The process of cocooning is eminent to our survival. It is paramount to implement if we are to successfully survive and thrive. My sister often reminds me that "sleep is spiritual", and it is. Suspira. The process of powering down and being or getting in tune with self is necessary and it becomes part of your self care. People will often try to make us believe that in doing so, or any number of things that are self preserving, that we are ultimately being selfish. Reject that guilt! Whatever with that bull*. Cocoon and embrace. It is part of the butterfli lifestyle. It is part of the butterfli mindset.

To further demonstrate the essence and culture of cocooning, it is when you, to an extent, shut yourself off from the world or whomever. It does not have to be that extreme, because the point of cocooning is to regenerate your energy. Sometimes, we are so giving to others and things, in general, that we allow ourselves to be drained emotionally, spiritually, as well as mentally and physically. Allowing this self depletion, permits illness and disease to enter the mind, body, and soul. Sleep. Be still. BE quiet. Learn to listen to your inner voice. Promote peace within yourself and again, protect your energy at all costs. In the butterfly world, the cocooning stage is a state of rebirth, metamorphosis, change. It is the stage when the caterpillar reemerges as the butterfly. Cocoon, dammit! Embrace.

Example; I was healing from the heartbreak of a relationship. I needed to power down and reflect on what went wrong. I drank some wine (optional), took a spiritual bath (also optional) , did not answer phone calls or texts, looked at some movies, journaled (essential) and slept. I am sure there was some crying in there but either way my body and mind purged. Bad energy was purged until it was replaced by regenerative energy.

In your cocooning, give your mind time to rethink and analyze, dream. Many times, we receive clarity in our dreams. Something that we could not solve awake, can sometimes be resolved in the dream world. It is a reality and dimension that does exist.

On a metaphysical level, cocooning allows the body to regenerate and to heal. Cells are able to replenish. Toxins are cleared. Calmness reemerges and sustains. Powering down our bodies and minds provides the opportunity for our biorhythms to realign. Some may even say, chakra alignment. The benefits from the practice are endless. Make it a part of your repertoire. It is part of the butterfly (butterfli) lifestyle and the butterfly (butterfli)mindset.

Universe, Teach Me

What am I supposed to learn from what I experienced? That is what I often ask myself after I have experienced some things. What was experienced may be disappointing, dangerous, or daunting. What was I meant to learn from that? That is my prayer. That is the thought I am sending to The Universe as I seek answers. Those are the questions that I am asking God. I also want to add that to me and for me, God goes by many names. Thus, when I refer to the Universe, it is God within connectedness. Some of my elders do not like for me to say Universe, and think that I am not revering God. Well, when they write their own book they can use the language of their choosing and understanding. I, the butterfli that I am, commune with God, i.e., The Universe, in the way that befits me and I implore each of you to do the same. I'll speak on that later, in more context, when we delve into the chapter concerning spirituality.

So, we have a set of experiences. I refrain from believing that coincidences exist. I refrain from believing that things 'just happen'.

Our experiences are based on the choices we make as well as Divine energy. Just as in 'The Butterfly Effect' movie, the theory is presented that one set of actions causes another set of actions. To take that further, things do happen for a reason. We do not always understand that reason. Additionally, some things happen as a reaction to some action that we have taken or chosen. Either way, when we experience certain events, such as a heartbreak or we meet someone that aligns with goals that we may have been thinking but stagnant in our action, the Universe will provide either the opportunity or the result for us to either reflect or move forward with the situation that presents. It is the opposite of coincidence.

I have said before that energy is everything. It is in the actions we take or do not take. It is in our thoughts. That is why we have to constantly feed our minds that benefits our souls and protects our energy. Thus, is my prayer, "Universe, Teach me. Please teach me what I am supposed to learn from this so that I will refrain from living this part of my journey over again."

Metamorphosis

"The process of transformation is not about becoming something that we weren't. It's about reinventing what we were the whole time."
- **Author William Paul Young**

If there is one thing that I have learned in my Butterli journey is never be afraid to reinvent yourself. It doesn't need to be anything that is planned or premeditated. It can be the natural path flow of your journey and culmination of your experiences. What does that mean? That may mean changing your name, changing your geographic location, changing your career path, changing partners, circles, or even belief systems. Your metamorphosis is uniquely yours. And, while that may sound like a bunch of words, there is much meaning in those words, and you just have to make the choice to take heed to them. I have at one time or another, done each and all of those. When a marriage did not work for me, I changed direction. When I needed to redefine myself for myself, I did so, regardless of others' thoughts. You have to allow yourself that metamorphosis, that transformational energy to take place. Doing so, is what butterflies do. And no, transformational energy is not gender specific, so if thinking in terms of being a butterfly, know that there are male and female butterflies as well as their not so distant cousin, the dragonfly.

Just as the butterfly stages from; egg, caterpillar, pupa, adult, we transform and metamorph through our different stages and experiences. Butterfliology is the combination of science and spirituality. Is it a religion? No, but it is a lifestyle. It is a mindset.

The Lay
Of The Land

Get to know your surroundings. Be cautious and or cautiously optimistic when entering into a new situation, job, circle, without revealing too much of yourself or what you are about until you get to observe and know the players and the lay of the land. I have learned and experienced this from an array of viewpoints. The knowledge and wisdom obtained from this is for example, when you begin a new job, the most important part for you to remember is to listen, observe, and listen some more. The truth is you do not know who is sleeping with who, who is married to who, who is related to who, who went to school with who, who has worked with who before, and on and on...

You are the new kid on the block and you don't really know sh* yet. And, even if you have all the knowledge in the world, do not let all that energy spill and burst at once. Hold your cards, and most importantly hold your tongue. And, if you truly feel that you need to vent, take it outside of anyone working at your job. Venting to someone at work, that you have not established a solid, trusting relationship with is the fastest way to destroy your work situation. You will most likely get blamed for what you did and did not say, and because you are the new kid in town, there may not be anyone to vouch for you. People do not like a know it all. Allow your knowledge to seep in. Allow them to observe and ingest exactly who you are and what you bring to the table. Following this rule or advice, will definitely make everything a lot easier for you and vitally increase your success. It will also give you an advantage because people will trust you more when and if they see that you are not a busy body or quick to tell yours or anyone else's business.

Example: A family member started a new job. She, of course, wanted to do and give her best. So, she worked harder than anyone in the immediate company, even her own supervisor. She learned her job in half the time. She exhibited her ability to be detail oriented and she did this in an expedient amount of time. Before you know it, she was asking for things to do, because she was finishing the assignments quicker than they could crank them out. Well, someone took offense to that. Instead of being praised for what she knew, her abilities, her dedication, she was pushed out of the organization. In fact, one co worker told her that she needed to slow down and she was completing the work too fast. What was the problem with avid productivity, you might ask? Well, if the other ones that were there before you were 'pacing themselves' and you come in there like a bolt of lightning and zoom through everything, that presents a problem for them and may very well bring into question their productivity standards. In other words, in their eyes, whether unknowingly or unintentionally or not, she made them look bad, feel inferior, or was just a show off. Why are people like that? Why do people try to keep us within a box of their comfort of choosing? Why are some people threatened by our shine? Smh. Horrible right? Horrible, but true. Therefore, the lesson in that for you is to get to know the lay of the land. It is for your benefit. It is a survival tool. In this life, we want to do more than survive. We want to survive and thrive, but in order to do that, you have to be smart. You have to be clever and know when to hold what you know. Utilize your knowledge when it benefits you and observe, observe, listen and observe.

In all truth and honesty, that was not the right setting for her. She would have been stifled there. However, losing significant income in a time frame that did not allow her to control the narrative placed her in a state of perpetual dependence that she had to fight her way out (of). It was a hard lesson to learn but it was a lesson that The Universe taught her before she landed in a career that she really, really liked. The lessons that she learned from that situation helped prepare for success in her next situation because she took heed to the lessons that she learned. Thus, The Universe did not need to teach them again.

Butterfli Thought

"Sometimes, our light is brighter than we even realize. Others recognize it before you do."

- J. Azules Amor

Energy Is Everything

"As a man thinketh"
- **Proverbs 23:7**

Energy is in everything. It is in all animate and inanimate objects. I cannot emphasize enough the importance of protecting your energy but to also be aware of your energy and the energy around you.

Clutter blocks our energy. It changes the energy flow. I have experienced this for myself, and noticed that when I feel chaotic, my room or living space reflects that. When my thoughts begin to clear, and I am coming close to a resolution, I begin cleaning, purging, clearing the clutter. Journaling helps with this process. I recommend journaling highly. It cleanses the spirit and opens the palette for more creative energy to flow. Purging is an integral part of the during and after cocooning process.

Some may say, how can an inanimate object hold energy? It's just a thing, right? That is not true. I'll take your memory back to the movie, 'The Golden Child' starring Eddie Murphy. That entire movie was based on the energy principle. Do you remember the little boy that was held in the box and they surrounded him on all four sides with negative energy around the clock to block his good energy? They used the bad energy as a way to control the boy and his energy. In fact, they tried to weaken his energy by tricking him into eating things that would go against his belief system and weaken his energy. The boy was very smart and protected his energy at all costs. He respected the power of energy. His enemies were also aware of energy's power and presence and tried to use it to their advantage and his disadvantage. Energy was respected as the entity that it is.

With that being said, please protect your energy. You can do this through awareness. Be in tune with your instincts. Once again, Butterfliology is both science and spiritual. To an extent, it is the metaphysical manifestation of thoughts and actions. Butterfliology is a mindset. It is a lifestyle.

I find it important, pertinent even, to have your tribe, your circle. It is imperative that you keep a circle around you with those that can replenish your energy and there is a practice of constant and consistent reciprocation. The reciprocal, the act of reciprocity should be part of your ongoing repertoire. It should come natural in your circle. In building your circle, you eventually build your tribe. Your tribe consists of those who cheer you own and are genuinely concerned about your well being and happiness. They impart knowledge and everyone is comfortable with everyone else's 'shine'. I have different circles and within those circles, your core group is formed, and eventually becomes your tribe.

Respect Energy. Be aware and harness it.

Mentorship

I cannot emphasize enough the importance of engaging in mentorship. It is important to both have a mentor as well as to mentor others. In fact, the practice of mentorship sometimes involves having multiple mentors, as each one can offer a different perspective or offer different talents or experiences that may help guide you.

It is important to both have a mentor as well as to mentor others. In fact, the practice of mentorship sometimes involves having multiple mentors, as each one can offer a different perspective or offer different talents or experiences that may help guide you.

In the spirit of 'Each one Teach One', your experiences can also be beneficial to others to help them on their journey. You may not feel that you have something to offer or that your experiences matter, but the truth is mentoring others helps you be a better mentee.

When you can, help someone help someone. Knowledge does no good if we keep it all to ourselves. The same can be said of our experiences. Perhaps your journey, your butterfli path, led you to certain experiences and challenges, to allow you the opportunity to assist others. Oftentimes, our journey is not solely about ourselves, but it is also in the service of others. I truly believe that.

I can tell you that I know now, although I did not know then, that a portion of my journey was meant for the service of others. This is why I can let you know about "The Lay of the Land" because I have seen it and experienced it. If my journey can somehow enhance your journey, then it was worth it.

We cannot keep the knowledge and benefit of experience solely to ourselves. It is our duty to guide others. And, as much knowledge and we earn and learn, there is always more to learn. Part of the journey of mentorship is acknowledging those who have and continue to make a difference in our lives and to acknowledge that no one knows everything. We have to allow for mistakes for ourselves as well as others' mistakes, and to know that as long as we are doing the best that we can and coming from a place that is pure of heart, we can do the most good.

When we do not know something, acknowledge that. Do what you can to get the answer. Be solutions oriented. There is nothing wrong with venting or expressing, within the right context, but also be solutions oriented. Asking yourself, "What can I do to resolve this situation?" BE about that business. See that in others and see that in yourself. That way you know that you are on the right path to mentoring. active mentorship, and being mentored by others via wise counsel.

Keep in mind that mentors come in all shapes, sizes, ages, and walks of life. You can learn from youth as well as elders. A college education is not the defining factor in mentorship. Neither is age. The

Divine imparts knowledge to whom He chooses. Please keep in mind that Experience is the greatest teacher. Read, listen, observe. BEnefit from others' experience and perspectives. It will serve you well.

Don't Activate My Crazy

Why? Why must you activate my crazy, and why must you insist on doing so? This is sometimes the question that you have to ask. It is for the times when that certain someone insists on 'trying you' and then acting so surprised when your crazy emerges. Really? Are you really surprised though? Because I gave you a complete disclosure statement and you also acknowledged it when you told me that I was crazy. In fact, you said, "...you are crazy. You are good and crazy. But, I like a little crazy." These were your words. So, then you do shyt that activates my crazy and then act like I have done something wrong. Smh. That, is the exact definition and epitome of a 'smh' moment. Help us, Oh God.

So, I am going to say to my ladies, why do the fellas (or whomever you love) insist on doing things that are going to eventually bring us out of our character and emerge as our alter ego? Why, when they know how sweet and loving, caring, and considerate we can be, take us there? We try not to go there, right? Who wakes up and wants to have a Jazmine Sullivan moment or who cannot relate to a Jill Scott, "calling too damn much" moment? WE have all been there at one time or another or another. Why do they insist on having us re enact our Julia Roberts character on 'Something to Talk About' because we told them there would be the day? Cardi says, "BE careful with me." But they insist on being hard headed, not taking heed, ignoring the warning signs, walking into danger, and in some situations, just being completely and totally disrespectful?! I am going to add to that. Disrespectful, dismissive, and rude. Oooooh, now that's what gets me! Especially when we have already told them AND demonstrated a taste of crazy in other scenarios.

In my situation, I try to talk to her. I try to talk to that side of me and keep her calm. Sometimes, we will have whole and complete conversations trying to mitigate the risks of the behavior we know we are capable of exhibiting but try to refrain from doing so.

"You know I don't do the things with others that I do with you, that you and I do, so why you gon' act like that?" These are the questions. leading up to the event. It is an event of their choosing that hopefully won't formulate into a Left Eye moment, but know she did not get to that moment by herself. There were signs, talks, tears, and warnings. "Please don't take my love for granted." That's all we are really saying. This all culminates into...please don't activate my crazy.

Butterfli thought:

"There is a crazy bytch that lives inside of me. Please don't activate her."

- J. Azules Amor

Butterfli Journey/ Self Discovery

"All things work together for good for those who love the Lord and are called according to His purpose."
- Romans 8:28

In the Self Discovery process as part of your Butterfli Journey all sorts of changes and experiences shape who you are and who you are to become.

If we do live more than once, we only remember one life at a time. Thus, make the best of that life and live it to the fullest. As the saying goes, YOLO, (popularized by Drake, and for me 'Scandal') and live it abundantly.

What does that mean and how does that translate into our everyday lives one may ask? Make decisions that are good for you. Seek guidance from reliable counsel. As far as your self discovery journey, you will metamorph many times while on your path. Embrace that. Own that. It is a journey that is solely and uniquely yours. We don't know why we have certain experiences. We do not always understand the purpose in our experience, although at some point, we come to the understanding that it makes and forms us into who we are.

People that know me say that I am hard on myself, that I am very self determined and "driven". I also hear in the observance of the Johari Window that I have very high standards. These are observations that I have learned to accept as Truths in my Johari Window.

The Johari Window consists of four views, very similar to a window pane. How do you see yourself? How do others see you?

The key is to take the knowledge from the Johari Window and allow it to enhance your self discovery, self journey process and know they are all part of the pieces or the puzzle that encompasses who you are.

Within this journey, you may, after analysis, meditation, and mentoring, and prayer, choose to make some changes to your Johari. That is perfectly fine. We all do that from time to time. As long as you are being true to your Divine self, those kinds of changes and acknowledgements can be necessary and healthy. The key in self discovery is to retrain from being what and who others want you to be, to refrain yielding solely to their desires, if they are in opposition to your true spirit and what you want for and of yourself.

If you do not have an idea or clue as to who you are and what you want from your journey, take some time to meditate, pray, journal, and cocoon to become in tune with your true self and your desires. When seeking counsel, I can only stress the need for wise counsel. You will know this by the fruits of their spirit, their actions, and your inner being (that quiet voice, or First Mind). Trust that energy to lead you on your discovery.

As it pertains to believing in ourselves, we don't have to have it all figured out, but it starts with a dream. You can envision your success and manifest it into your life. When in doubt, I have to remember that Spike Lee believed in himself so much that he financed his first film entirely off his credit cards. When in doubt, I have to remember that Tyler Perry started out homeless and sleeping in his car...but he had a dream and believed in himself.

We cannot allow the fear of failure to take over. We have to take chances and we have to believe. We have to have the belief so strongly that the power to succeed is stronger than the fear of anything else. We have to be so determined in our souls and in our spirits that we seek the light and hold onto that hope when we are weary. We have to believe that there is a destiny in our life beyond our understanding.

Butterfli Thought

"Sometimes, people are drawn to your energy because they are hungry,"

- J. Azules Amor

OPEN SELF

(Known to you and others)

HIDDEN SELF

(Known to you but not known to others)

BLIND SELF

(Known to others but not self)

UNKNOWN SELF

(Not known to you or others)

Spirituality

"Your church is where you are. You hold church everyday. Your temple is where you are."

- Patsy Thomas

Spiritual baths are a good thing to bring yourself into alignment. Burning Sage is good for clearing out old energy along with scripture or and prayer. Candles, incense, and spiritual baths are essential habits to integrate into your regular self care regimen. To be clear, there are baths for cleansing the body and there are baths for soul cleansing. Your spiritual advisor should be able to submit a recipe that will assist you in achieving your goal. Whenever I am off center and I need to realign with my energy, my spiritual advisor has posed the question, "Have you taken a spiritual bath lately?

The idea of a personal altar came to me through seeing friends who practiced Buddhism and Santeria. It is a practice that I will soon incorporate in my daily life and space. You do not need to prescribe to a certain or particular belief to incorporate this practice into your daily life and space. It is a way to focus and meditate on your own spirituality and spiritual needs.

Be obedient to your spirit. When you have an idea or a name of a loved one or thought that continues to present itself, yield and take heed. Be obedient to your spirit. There is no such thing as coincidence, and those who refer to such refrain from great understanding. Be in tune with your spirit and be obedient.

Vibrations, as a form of energy that you can feel and can direct you and guide you. It is a spiritual rhythm. Energy creates other energy. For example, the first time I was invited to Buddhisht chanting, I could feel the power of the vibrations. The rhythmic words, together, the wavelength that was created, in turn created more energy. Music generates certain feelings and emotions from us and it is a spiritual language. It evokes a certain energy, and that is why you must be careful and conscious as to what energies you allow, musical, people, others vibrations, or otherwise. It all works together.

Release the strongholds that bind you to whatever negative force that may be omnipresent in your life. Pray for this release and the strength to overcome those challenges in your Divine path or journey.

Feed your spirit good things. Our spirits need to be fed constantly, just as our bodies and our minds. This is why some people choose to read the Quran, the Bible, the Tanakh, the Torah, the Tripitaka, or the holy teachings that coordinate directly with their faith. The same can be said of positive affirmations, inspiring stories or personal testaments. It's the same concept of filling a pitcher of water that becomes empty from giving. You have to constantly and consistently fill your spirit with things that will provide it new life and energy.

When you feed someone else, you are feeding your spirit also. We learn and receive by giving to others. That is why there is such a fulfillment in providing knowledge to others. In providing to others, you indirectly are feeding your spirit through the joy that others' receive.

Replenish the spirit of those who help guide you. We probably do not give much thought to our spiritual leaders or mentors needing their spirits to be filled or replenished because we seek answers from them. We think of them as God's vessels and somehow, superhuman, and above the fray. Nothing could be further from the Truth. Just because they have a special connection with the Higher Power, does not stop them from having real world problems, pains, disappointments, concerns. Consider that they may need someone to listen to them, offer them a kind word, provide them with wisdom that feeds their spirit. By replenishing their energy, you are also indirectly giving back to others as well as yourself.

Some people say that superstitions do not exist...that they are not real? But, do they though? I am not suggesting that anyone allows their lives to be ruled by superstitions or anything that holds you captive in bondage. However, in my experience, a person's perception is influenced by its name. For example, in a conversation with my spiritual advisor, I asked him why I seemed to think things at a stronger frequency than ever before and why did it happen to me more and more frequently? His advice was that I was more in tune with my true nature and more accepting to who and what I am. It makes sense, because as a little girl I used to have dreams that would come true. That scared me. I did not know what it was or how to harness it, so I asked God to take that gift away from me. I believe, just as the opening quote in 'Metamorphosis',

"The process of transformation is not about becoming something that we weren't. It's about unveiling what we were the whole time."
- **Author William Paul Young**

So, in that, take it for what is worth to you. It is up to each individual to decide for themselves their spiritual trajectory. Some believe that to be Christian, you can only embrace that one teaching and you have to reject all others. To that, I say, you have to make spirituality your own, no matter what your belief and in my mind's eye, I embrace a bevy of beliefs to form my own spirituality. I refrain from allowing religion to define me and I embrace the various spiritual teachings from my many friends that beliefs vary from mine. Yet, in all of the variance, I find that the core belief is the same and the fruit draws what is inside of you just as spoken in 'The Law of Attraction' . This frequency happens whether we realize it or not.

Another wise word is where you choose to worship. I grew up Southern Baptist, the granddaughter of a preacher. I lived with my grandparents for many years, so I was brought up as one of their own children. We went to church every Sunday following Sunday School and Devotion. Most Sundays there was either Sunday evening service or going to a visiting church. During the week there was Bible study, choir rehearsal, visiting the sick and shut in, and annual Revival Service, which may take place throughout the year if we participated in the revival services of other churches also. There was also Communion which involved washing of the feet, just like John the Baptist, Vacation Bible School, Southern Baptist Conferences, and if you were on the choir, you may sing lead songs or sing solos at local churches, as well as Welcome Speeches. Suspira. Yes, going to church, religion was a huge core part of your growing up. Anything outside of that was blasphemous. Surely, I am forgetting something. In addition to these things, I was also a soloist, so I sang and performed 'The Creation' by James Weldon Johnson at visiting churches where my grandfather would preach. There is no wonder why you find some of the most awesome talent trained and brought up in the church. Oh yes, I almost forgot about church plays, especially at Christmas, when my Black babydoll was Jesus laying in the manger.

I am sure that many of you can relate to what I just described, especially in the Black community. Most of us grew up in church, and it was an integral part of our lives. I can definitely see the value in what I have learned and my experiences. I am thankful for that goodness that was instilled in me. From those experiences, I have formulated what works for me and my life.

The point is, although I grew up in a very traditional belief system, as I became into my own as an adult, I had to define what spirituality meant to and for me. I respect all belief systems. It is up to each of us, individually, to decide what that means for us and what that looks like.

You are now entering the introduction of the second book in the Butterfliology series; Butterfliology: Butterflies, Butterflies, and Dragonflies Too. It is my hope and intent that you partake and that it benefits those who both receive and absorb these messages. I am a portal. The messages within are a result of me following my spirit and being obedient to it as it reaches the someone or someones for which it is intended.

Amen Ashe'

PREVIEW

Butterfliology:
Butterflies, Butterflies, and Dragonflies Too

Darkest Before The Dawn 83
Males Have Feelings Too 87
There's No Such Thing As Coincidence 91
Pain And Purpose 95
Purging 103
Friends Should Have Contracts Too. 107
Sometimes, We Don't Know Why We're... 111
Candles 115
Guys: From Friends To Lovers. 119
Being A Light Giver. 123
Do What Makes Your Heart Happy. 127
Be Your Authentic Self And Be True To Who You Are. 131
Synesthetes, Empaths, And Seers 137
Talent, Gifts, And Languages 143
Prayer 149

BUTTERFLIOLOGY

Acknowledgements/Thank Yous 151
Reflective Thoughts 153
Reflective Questions 159
Johari Window 167
Resources 175

Darkest Before The Dawn

Have you ever noticed how right when you're on the precipice of your blessings trouble, doubt, sadness, and/or life's challenges hit the hardest? I have. That has happened to me several times throughout my life and on several occasions on the eve of some very important events or milestones in my life. One of the most recent is right after completing this book. Literally, the next day after completing this book, I experienced this immense sadness. I was crying, unsure if I wanted to go on, and just felt this engulfing sadness. I was literally so very elated the day before, and texted everyone that I was finally finished with my book creation. Everyone was shocked when the next day I texted my immense sadness. I have seen and experienced the times in my life when things would get so heavy in life and problems would hurl themselves at you with such great ferocity that it left your wondering. My spiritual advisor reminded me on more than one occasion that trouble didn't last always and that it was often darkest before the dawn. In my observances of life, I have found that to be true. I know that in my situation, the spirit world enemy was angry. My message was complete and ready to go out into the world. It was what we hear elders refer to as being under spiritual attack. Experiencing that also allowed me to know that I was onto something special. It was confirmation that my message needed to be heard. I know more than ever before that it was my duty to put this message out into the world and it needed to be heard. It was my spiritual confirmation that others could benefit from what was being released from my soul. My spiritual energy was the vessel of The Divine and I needed to be obedient.

I have learned more and more to listen and be obedient to my spirit. It's amazing that what I thought were journal entries originally meant for me were really messages that were twofold in that they were for me but were also for the world. Someone needs to hear this message. Someone needs to hear what I have to say and it is my duty to oblige and be obedient to my spirit, my Divine.

The message to you, coupled with my experience is yes, it does get darkest before the dawn. Stay faithful and remain strong on your spiritual journey of Faith. Follow your spirit's path and stay steadfast in prayer and mediation. Listen to your spirit. And as Rev. James Brown, in his James Cleveland voice says, "Trouble don't last always." So, if you can pray your way through it and go with your spirit, instead of your focus being against your spiritual enemy, you can survive through the darkness.

Males Have Feelings Too

Growing up, I didn't see men cry. I don't even think men talked about or expressed their feelings. Fears were associated with femininity. The men that were in tune with their feelings were referred to as sissies and stripped and shamed of their masculinity. It wasn't until deep into my adulthood that I realized that this was all wrong and how much those messages, spoken or unspoken, affected me and affected my intimate relationships. I believe, over time, I began to treat men according to this stereotype and I could be quite harsh in my assessment. Over time, I became harsh and callous towards men and from their cruelty and callousness that I received. Vulnerability became much harsher in some aspects and I mastered the art of making a man feel like shyt. After all, they didn't have feelings anyway, right?

I believe that some men also believed and prescribed to the bullshyt that men didn't have feelings, emotions, fears, or vulnerability. I remember even thinking on at least one occasion that a man's tears weren't real. You never know how the messages you receive in your childhood affect and shape your perceptions and relationships.

It was in my experiences with a former lover that he opened my eyes to males' vulnerability. He expressed to me, on occasions, that I was completely insensitive, at times, to his feelings. He was right. There were times when I was in the complete spirit of being a bytch and I didn't care. My mouth was like an arsenal; the tool and weapon that I had developed and perfected over the years, came out full force. It was a combination of a defense mechanism and preconceived notions and observances that stemmed from childhood, past relationships, and what I had experienced from males who had inadvertently prescribed to that same bullshyt growing up. They had perceived many of those same defining messages that led them astray in their intimate relationships as well as how they treated, perceived, and presented themselves.

In this revelation, males have to give themselves permission to be men with emotions. They have to define themselves for themselves. Butterfliology. It's free thought. Males, seeing themselves as men, as human beings, entities with both feminine and masculine energies in balance of their dominant. I have both energies but feminine is my dominant.

I believe if people learn to embrace their Truth much earlier in life, the world would have a lot more happy people in it, less depressions, sadness, disappointment, more creativity and the ability to help in serving others as well serving themselves first.

There's No Such Thing As Coincidence

Coincidence does not exist. When people say coincidence they are refuting The Divine. When you look on your phone and see double or triple numbers that is not coincidence. When you've been thinking strongly of calls or texts you or shows up, that is the opposite of coincidence. In the chapter titled 'Energy is Everything' we talk about how energy is everything. When people realize how powerful energy is and how there is an energy element in everything

A mother wakes up or feels compelled to call her son or daughter because they feel something. It's that energy connection. People often doubt it, doubt what comes natural when we deny what is innate and intuitive. Society encourages embracing only what is scientific or what can be proven and refraining from reality that is metaphysical because of the spiritual element. Furthermore, people are discouraged from both talking about it or acknowledging it. You must always embrace and acknowledge the spiritual.

There are so many examples. Another example is when you meet someone through what seems like coincidence for a completely different purpose but then you realize you have so much in common. You seem like you've known that person for quite awhile or the energy flow is so natural and effortless. You'll realize that your circle, your tribe, or both has so many similarities, whether geographical commonalities or otherwise. That's why in the Santeria religion, for example, either uses certain beats or chords or refrains from listening to certain chords or beats rhythms because of the energies associated with them. I know for a fact that certain chords combined with beats compel a certain creative energy.

Just like in the Bible, answers can come to you in a dream. Dreams can be many things, including God's way of communicating to you or through you. You can be the vessel or portal for the message. That, in itself, can be your Divine purpose, For example, this book cover design came to me in a dream. Kozakura and I collaborated on the cover design for about three and a half weeks. She asked me a lot of questions to have me think about what I wanted as well as her getting a sense of what to create for the cover. I told her that I didn't know but I would pray on and for the answer. I prayed on it and it vividly came to me in a dream! I immediately wrote down everything I remembered about the dream in vivid detail including the butterfly positioning, colors, cosmic, metaphorical thought explosion feel, to the profile view and full lips of the Black woman thinking. Kozakura put her own interpretation of my mind's eye according to what I described and the cover design was born.

Dreams are important communication, just as prayers, walks, journaling, or meditations. They each provide you an opportunity to commune with your Divine Higher Power. The most important thing is the practice of being obedient when spiritually led and do a spiritual barometer check to make sure you are being led by the right spirit.

Pain And Purpose

"There is an opportunity in every obstacle."
- Dr. T. Battle

Pain and purpose is such a multi layered subject that requires a very delicate approach. Usually, I delve right in...straight, no chaser, but I have to keep in mind those that experience or have experienced such deep levels of pain that to suggest purpose in that would be almost irresponsible and callous at best. With that said and a fully present acknowledgement, in some instances, there can be purpose that is derived from one's pain.

For the longest time, I did not know or understand why I would experience certain things. "Why me God?" I'd ask. Tears streaming. I truly did not understand. And yes, I do understand Karma. However, as I think back, "Did I do something to deserve this in some way? Did I harm someone? Is this my tribulation for my past sins?" But the truth is, in some instances, our pain and what we experience through it is to help someone else in their journey. Sometimes, we are (to be) the testament as well as the beacon of hope for others. Sometimes, there is a lesson that we can apply to a future circumstance. When and if we receive the lesson, perhaps we can move on from that lesson. This is especially true if we've learned a lesson from our experiences. When we can explicate what it is that we have learned or perhaps even do differently, then our pain and purpose can be utilized to help others.

I believe I came into this knowledge when I realized that there was pain in purpose to many of the things I experienced. In retrospect, I understand that I am a spiritual portal. In that, there are things that I needed to experience to be in a position to help or guide others.

One of the things with pain and purpose is I used to wonder why I had to grow up in three places? Why could I never just give a simple answer when someone would ask where I was from when many people could just give a one or two word answer? No, my answer had to be more complicated or intricate than that. "I grew up in North Carolina, N.E. (North East) Washington, D.C. and the Bay Area, I would say. Damn. Why this shyt have to be so complicated? Smh. It would annoy me at times. I did not have the experience of having one set of childhood friends, going to the same high school or elementary school throughout my academic career or living in the world of one or two word answers. I later began to appreciate those experiences and embraced what made and makes me different. Growing up in those three places gives me a unique flavor and perspective. I am able to groove and move differently in different circles because I did have such a diverse upbringing. All of this stemmed from my grandmother's passing and my mother moving to D.C. to find better opportunities when I was two. These were two very significant factors that changed my life's course and journey. The purpose in that pain is that it made me into a very well rounded individual. I am thankful for growing up and my experiences in Cali. Fairfield, California to be exact.

I began traveling to the west coast from Concord, North Carolina when I was around 7 or 8. I formed a lifelong friendship with a girl named Quita, known affectionately as Felicia Roberts. She is one of my best friends. This same friend that I met at 7 or 8 used to let me stay in her dorm room at times when needed when she attended Howard University. My teenage years were challenging and at times, I would not have a place to stay. The irony is that we met as children on the other side of the country. Who would have known that would evolve into a lifelong friendship where we encouraged and continue to encourage each other through life's journey? Thus, the pain I endured there was a more prominent blessing in our meeting. When Felicia's mom transitioned from her earthly presence, I was right there at her graduation, cheering her on. Had the events and circumstances of the orginal pain not happened, as in my grandmother's earthly transitioning, I probably would have stayed in Concord forever, to be near her. I loved her just that much. My entire life course would have been different. Better? Worse? Whose to say that. The trajectory certainly was different and heavily influenced by the chain of events that took place. This book may have never been written and God may have not been able to use me to get the message to others. Pain and purpose.

Another lifelong friendship that was formed was from my gyurl Daphne Love Jones. Isn't that quite a name? She, Quita, and I all went to high school together in Fairfield. We partied at a spot in the Bay called The Caribee as well as various house parties including Vallejo, California. For the locals we refer to that as Valley Joe (pronunciation) and hanging out in the hills (Oakland Hills). Daphne and I have been there for each other with our children, relationship experiences, and I have helped her navigate through some situations in which I had a particular expertise and vice versa. Her mom had a daycare and was caregiver for my children. That may not seem like a big deal, but anyone that has children knows how challenging it can be to find reliable, safe, and quality daycare. It provides peace of mind to know someone is taking good care of your precious cargo, your hearts. When Daphne's mom earthly transitioned, it was natually one of the hardest times in her life, and I know that I served as an anchor in some aspect during her healing process. We are cosmically connected. Same birthdays. Same date. Same year. As I said, I do not believe in coincidence. Do you know how rare it is to find someone who has a birthday with same date and the same year and you are still friends from high school? Without delving into the full scope of our journey, I hope that you can connect these examples to your own lives. Pain and purpose.

For my peeps in D.C., my old stomping grounds are Brentwood, Edgewood and Saratoga. I attended McKinley Tech for a while and met one of my best friends, Stephanie L. Smith. She and her family took me under their wing and have been there for me in some of the most crucial times in my life. Knowing her has been life changing. She helped me get reacclimated to D.C. when I moved back from both North Carolina and California. She was a lifesaver following both divorce one and divorce two. When I had to travel to a completely different region for my custody battle, she and her mother watched over and cared for my children. She is a creative soul who has blessed my spirit with the honor of having met her. She helped me navigate through learning protocols with each of my sons and helped open their world to new possibilites. Without delving into each piece of our journey, I hope that you can relate this to some aspect of your life with the mindset of pain and purpose. She has been an angel who has helped me on my journey.

A few years ago, I lost one of my dearest childhood friends, Tonja Grier Okoye, She suddenly transitioned and left this earthly space at a very young age. It was not anticipated. That shook me. We were childhood friends from North Carolina and had known each other all our lives. We attended Winecoff Elementary together until I moved back to both Cali and D.C. It is still a challenge to think about or talk about these days but I wanted to share with you a deeper sense of both who I am and personal examples in pain and purpose. This beautiful soul who was always more than willing to give to others and made sure to celebrate my presence whenever I would come into town, showed me life's precious fragility. We had conversations between me, her and God but she showed me to appreciate life in a different way. I have seen what a broken spirit can do and I try to remember life's blessings. Pain and purpose.

Each of these ladies has had or has a pivotal role in my life which formulated into important roles in my development from childhood to adulthood. They were childhood or school friends that helped me in some of the most challenging times in my life and in various ways. Each experience and encounter helped shape and influence my life. In the same vain, there are times when I was able to be there for them in their journey.

If anyone grew up in any one of those three places, you know how absolutely different they are. I often joke to those who know me about how my accent changes according to each of those regions, depending on what I am feeling at the time. If I were a mixed drink, I'd be like a little bit of Southern Comfort mixed with Hennesey and Gin.

North Carolina is that foundation for me that gave me my religious strength and work ethic. I grew up on a farm there with my grandparents. Church every Sunday and through the week.

D.C. gave me that survival instinct and strength. I learned to navigate through the girl gangs at McKinley Tech at the time and to think strategically to a number of given situations, including choosing your battles and refraining from getting jumped. I also got a great big dose of Black pride and learning how a hood girl can formulate her own fashion sense and make a five and dime outfit look fresh off the runway.

Cali was those fun times that helped me find and define myself but also exposed me to diverse cultures and it is there I discovered so many different languages. In high school, I discovered my love and propensity for languages. My first language that I intensely learned was German. Frau Bailey was my instructor and somehow DLI tried to recruit me for their language program. Defense Language Institute. Although I excelled in German, there were not many opportunities to practice the language. I eventually switched to Spanish, which became a lifelong language for me. Living in California, which was originally Mexico, there were lots of second and third generation Spanish speakers in which I could practice and use my language skills. I learned how to relate to different people and the exposure to cultures I would not have otherwise known.

The point is in each of those experiences, there was purpose in the pain because it shaped who I am today. My painful experiences can serve to warn or help others. My knowledge can translate into messages to others and to assist them in their journey.

Of course that does not negate the pain from our experiences or even our desire to refrain from experiencing them in the first place.

Sometimes our pain is to bring us to a greater purpose. We don't know that at the time. It's only in retrospect that we are able to reflect on the pros, cons, and entirety of our experiences. Lastly, this is not to suggest that this explains every situation of pain. Sometimes, we may not ever know and for that I do not have the answer. This is to be taken in the context for which this applies.

Purging

Why do we hold onto old sh*? Screenshots? Old text messages? Visual voicemails, reminders of the past and bad memories? To do so gives it energy.

> *"When someone shows you who they are, believe them."*
> **- Dr. Maya Angelou**

Purging is omnipotent for both your physical and emotional space. Scientific studies have confirmed what I already knew: that your physical space is a representation of your mental and emotional state. Have you ever noticed when you're feeling extra chaotic and out of sorts, discombobulated and you just can't get it together that these are the times when your place is the messiest? or/and you're in a quagmire of constantly being late for work for a specific time frame? I'm not talking about those persons who are habitually late. That's a habit thing. I've been there too, and that consisted of me changing my habits. I'm talking about something different. When all of a sudden you can't seem to get it together or when you find yourself overlooking and living in chaos and just being in the habit of tucking it away. It's not until you begin coming out of the darkness, struggle, or chaos that you become able to begin organizing and clearing space. Your perspective changes and that paradigm opens up a channel that allows you to begin clearing your physical space; purging unneeded items and clearing your physical space. Remember when I said energy is everything? Animate and inanimate objects hold energy. And if you have too many objects cluttered and in your physical space you can block your good energy. Many times, we're holding on to things where a purge is needed and we don't even realize that purging is needed. I recently experienced a purge and it is ongoing. In my purge, I rid myself of eight large trash bags of items I donated to Goodwill and I'm still not done! Wtf?! Smh. I'm like what the f* have I been holding onto this stuff for? To help others? My original intent was to take many of those items back with me on my next visit to Cuba. Yes, my heart was in the right place but I wasn't doing what was best for me. I did not need all of that chaos in my physical space. Purge. Purge is the message of the day. Once I purged, my creative energy began to flow again effortlessly. Sometimes, we don't even realize why our energy is blocked. Recently, I realized I was holding onto mail from 2013, 2007. What?! Why?! OmG, so unnecessary. It's amazing that I managed to function in all that chaos. Purge and clear your energia. I am sure you'll feel better. You'll think more clearly and be able to problem solve.

Friends Should Have Contracts Too.

Just because you know someone does not mean business should happen without contracts and explicit understanding. Make sure people you hire are qualified and supervise their work too.

I came into this understanding when I helped someone I thought was a friend rehabilitate their credit. I made the mistake of not requiring payment first. It was my mistake, retrospectively, because the very reason the person needed my help in the first place is because they didn't pay their bills. They had jacked up credit. So, what was I thinking? I was thinking that I was helping a friend and that somehow they would treat me better than the creditors that had extended him credit. Wrong. I thought that the person respected me too much to ever violate me in such a way. Furthermore, I thought that because we knew each other since childhood and went way back that I could give this person more trust than most. Wrong again.

Additionally, because this was my friend, I went over and beyond in not only helping him rehabilitate his credit, I wrote letters to creditors, negotiated his student loan debt and payment arrangements, applied loan forgiveness options, and Cease and Desist letters. Would you like to know how my friend thanked me? Besides not paying me and ignoring my billing statement invoices, my friend eventually posted on his social media feed a picture of him with his spankin' brand new jeep that my hard work provided via his new and improved credit score. Yes, indeed. True story. And contrary to popular belief, it's not always easy to just to and sue someone to recoup your costs. The person must be served properly and you have to provide proof of your agreement.

Is it possible to do business with a friend successfully? Yes, but it's a gamble. Are you willing to take that risk? You know yourself. How well do you handle betrayal or perceived betrayal? I know I take betrayal as a cardinal sin. I am loyal to the end and anticipate the same from others. Therefore, if there is a situation of betrayal from someone I considered a friend, I take that shyt extra badly. It pierces. It hurts. It stings. It angers and it takes something from inside you. Even if it doesn't break your spirit, it kind of cracks at it a bit. It's definitely not something to be taken lightly. So much of the pain and confusion can be eliminated if you implement a contract. That way everyone is clear on their role and anticipations. Will this alleviate every mishap? Most likely not but it's definitely a step in the right direction and can avoid a lot of pain in the long run. Save yourself some heartache and lost time currency and consider a contract.

Sometimes, We Don't Know Why We're...

Attracted to certain things or people, when in fact, we're attracted to their energy. Two of the most seemingly unlikely people can share a connection. Although it may be inexplicable to others, the energies have connected on a spiritual level. In essence, we are spirits walking around interacting and existing everyday. That's why the mind is so powerful and we have the ability to change things and influence circumstances with thought. That is why it is essential to change or redirect the flow of energy when it becomes detrimental for us or no longer serving.

In the chapter called 'Energy is Everything' we spoke about energy and how everything has energy whether inanimate or animate. People will either be brought into your circle or repelled from the energy we carry. That's why it is also a challenge to break from certain people even when we have determined that they are neither good nor encouraging for us. It's that spiritual connection, and in those instances you may need to add rituals such as spiritual baths as well as exercise and prayer to help cleanse or dilute the connection. Sometimes, the connection remains but you eventually learn to manage it.

I have experienced this phenomenon in several instances, both romantic and otherwise. Energy is energy and it comes in all forms. Recently, I have experienced a connection so strong and me being drawn to the person that I didn't understand why journaling, exercising, praying to God, listening to music, and the other things I did to try and break the connection did not work. I realized we were connected on a cosmic level and that's why none of the other things worked.

Candles

With that said, I believe many of us underestimate the power and significance of candles as well as its spiritual connection and entity. In all religions and faiths the candle is a consistent and integral entity that holds, exposes, expels, gives, and breaks through barriers. When I am faced with troubles and confusion, my spiritual advisor always says, "I'll put up a light for you." I never really gave much thought to its significance until I began noticing a common theme in my shows such as 'La Rosa de Guadalupe' or 'Fools Rush In' or 'LoveCraft Country', 'Siempre Bruja' or countless other shows and religious programs. So, I began to give thought and pay closer attention to the significance and power of candles.

When I consulted with Rev. JB as to whether I was on the right path with writing about candles, it was confirmed that there was definitely an important viability. There are times that I doubt my first mind and I remind myself to be obedient to my spirit. After all, in writing this book, I was following my spirit and being obedient to it, even when I did not fully understand it at the time. Thus, he explained to me that candles pertain to the wavelengths that are produced and directly connects and influences the energies. Additionally, he elaborated that different color candles propel different energies and different purposes.

People are naturally drawn to candles for the metamorphic feelings they produce. It's another form or transformative energy and isn't that what we are all seeking in the end? A reflection or path to our higher selves, Whether we fully understand it or not, the message is to refrain from underestimating the power of candles. They have different meanings and purposes for everyone, but they are powerful entities all the same. The evidence is clear by their use in different religions and beliefs worldwide.

I know that when I need to emphasize a certain focus, I am drawn to light a candle. In my recent research, some attest to using candles with intention...but do we not all have intention of some sort when we light a candle? The next time you decide to light a candle, pay attention to how the candle light transforms your mood and state of being and respect it as its own connective entity.

Candles can be used for many purposes and your use and intent is personal. Candles can be used to draw someone closer to you, repel someone from you, for their aromatherapy purposes, to give focus, and to help illuminate a path during prayer or meditation. They can be used for evil or good. Either way, know the power of transformation that candles hold as their own spiritual energy and light source. Their transformative energy cannot be denied.

Guys: From Friends To Lovers.

Are you sure you want to f* that up? Do you really want to complicate things? Think carefully.

I know it's tempting to want to romantically partner with someone in which you both have something in common. From your viewpoint and culmination of experiences, that person is like your best friend and there is a certain comfortability that you haven't before experienced. You have flirted with the idea. Toggled with it in your mind and wondered if… You've played out different scenarios, sexually and otherwise. I can't tell you not to do it, but are you really sure though? Think about it. It's a gamble. Things could go beautifully and you live in the life of happily ever after. The other side of that is this entire thing could go terribly wrong. In this scenario, you could also lose everything; a friend and a lover. In the process of this romantic pursuit, you could lose your best friend and end up seeing the ugliest parts of each other. It's a gamble and you have to ask yourself...is it worth it? You have to decide that, but I can tell you that sex and romance changes everything. Before you make your final decision it would behoove you to visit and read my chapter called, 'Don't Activate my Crazy'. It's real. Once she experiences the heights of euphoria, your relationship has forever changed.

You can never talk with her about another woman in the same context as before. She is not going to want to share or even think about anyone experiencing what she's experienced or experiencing with you. Also, because you were friends first, she has all the keys to the castle and knows where all the bodies are dumped or buried, metaphorically speaking. You've expressed to her all your game moves with other chicks, and women never forget. I am not saying it cannot work but I am saying that it is a high probability that it may not be feasible and to really give it some true thought before pursuing that path. Equally so, you know all her secrets also. You have seen her 'play' men or how she reacts to different scenarios. Look at your decision from all angles and consider your outcomes very carefully. Once that line has been crossed, it's a done deal. The relationship will never be the same. My emphasis is are you really ready for that? Think carefully. If after considering all of that, you still want to delve into that situationship, then perhaps it is indeed the best decision for you.

Being A Light Giver.

There are professions and positions that impart knowledge and enlighten others; life coaches, teachers, preachers, coaches, counselors. You're always giving and imparting knowledge. Whether you realize or not, your purpose is to impart light to others. As noble as that is, you need to realize the depth of what you do, it's importance, and its effects on you. You must replenish your spirit regularly and consistently. You need to have a place or method to both mind and spiritual dump all the energies that you have absorbed while giving. You probably don't realize how much you're depleted because you have a natural inclination to give, share, and help others. You want to make others' lives better and will give until the point of self depletion.

Light givers are needed. They illuminate the world and prevent the world from falling into complete darkness. Similarly, if or when a light giver misuses his or her position, which is a position of power and instead of imparting light, imparts darkness, the impact is triple fold in devastation. Light givers have the ability to shape and change the world through their words, and actions which are their gifts. Similarly, there is an awesome responsibility and burden enlisted to and by a light giver. The seriousness, power, and responsibility that is held by a light giver must, as importantly, take care of themselves in and with the same way they take care of others.

Do What Makes Your Heart Happy.

"We know what we want as children. We often just give in to others' definitions of ourselves. Tradition ain't for everybody. Ignore the doubters. Depart from the non believers. Make your own path and be true to who you are."

- J. Azules Amor

One of the worst things you can do to yourself is to disallow yourself happiness by spending the majority of our time currency in a profession of job in which we are absolutely miserable. Remember, time is a currency. If we want others to respect our time currency, we must begin with ourselves. I know we all have to eat and we all have to survive. Your pursuit of happiness is not given in the spirit of refraining from common sense. You do what you need to do until you can do. What I am saying is refrain from being caught up in survival and denying yourself the benefit of thriving and true living. As you are working in your survival mode, do something to work on your dream everyday. Work towards your path. Envision your happiness.

Listen to encouraging messages. (See resources section First Edition, Butterfliology 'Free Thought'). Pray for guidance, if you do not know what your happy is. Just know that time is a currency. It is a currency that can never be given back and there are no refunds, so use your time wisely and give it wisely. Only give time to the things that are worthy of your intention. Do what makes your heart happy. Listen to your inner spirit, pray about it, act upon it.

Be Your Authentic Self And Be True To Who You Are.

"People will either accept you or not but as long as you love yourself and are true to who you are, you're on the right path."
- J. Azules Amor

Always be willing to learn from others. You can learn from your children. You can learn from your elders. You can learn from your peers. Be observant and listen. These are keys to your own personal success. Keep an open mind while diligently protecting your energy and being in the presence of wise counsel. The Bible says you will know people by their fruit. Dr. Maya Angelou says, "When someone shows you who they are, believe them." Being your authentic self involves barometer checks, but barometer checks of the soul. In other words, check in with yourself to see how you're doing and if you're in tune with what you're presenting. Change, in itself, is a constant metamorphosis and growth. It's cyclical. But you must make sure that what you are seeking or conforming stays true to the core of who you are. Otherwise, you're asking for unhappiness and ultimate disaster.

It's okay to be different. I always have been. Sometimes, you may feel that you don't belong until you embrace what makes you different. You have to believe in yourself so loudly that you echo out all the other voices, doubters, haters, and those that authenticate themselves as followers in lieu of being leaders.

I am a spiritual power.

I have gifts inside of me.

Gifts the world can see or feel

It is my desire to release what is special about me
and announce it proudly to the world,

I hold the peace inside of me that I am okay
with what and who I am.

- J. Azules Amor

"For my empaths, keep shining. Allow the world to glisten with your emotional, intuitive spirit guide. Trust your vibrations and continue to read those energies around you. Continue to protect your energy and trust your Divine instinct."

- J. Azules Amor

Synesthetes, Empaths, And Seers

There is a place for you. You are in the butterfli clan and it can often feel strange and lonely. It can feel like an impossible path because it's not easy being different. It's not easy carrying that spiritual burden, responsibility, or blessing, Depending on how you look at it, it can be one or a combination of all of those. I just want you to know, if you don't already, embrace your spiritual gifts and know that you are seen, heard, and recognized.

I first learned of synesthesia approximately three years, 2018 or 2017 and was astounded and completely fascinated by the phenomenon that there are people around us that see and taste colors. That there are people that see sound as colors and that everyone they encounter has a different vibrancy, aura, and spectrum of colors that they see per encounter. I find it fascinating. And yet, with all the scientific research and books, including Ted Talk(s)* that focus on the subject, it's still fairly unknown and unrecognized. What brought this back to my remembrance is the artist, Kozakura. Although we have never met in person or heard each other's voice, she was able to interpret my vision in such a way that the thought occurred, once everything was finished, that Kozakura was either a synesthete, or like me, an empath. I actually believe that...that just like one can be a combination learner, one can also be a combination of the above and have the abilities of a synesthete, empath, or seer.

As a little girl, I would have dreams and they would come true and that scared me. I asked God to take that gift away but what I learned is that gifts are never truly gone. Perhaps they are suppressed or evolve into something else but they are never truly gone. I also would have 'other worldly' dreams where I was in another world...literally another dimension. Yes, it was on this planet but it was somewhere in the Caribbean, for instance, or another country...I don't quite know. This happened on several occasions and I was known in that region, or wherever it was. We all had accents and spoke to each other in another language. In that setting, I was a seer. I know that realm is real. It exists. I have not been in that realm for a while but I am confident it exists. I believe dreams are spiritual communications, sometimes through galaxies. I am sure that I am not the first to have this thought, just the first one to say it aloud, outside of creative circles. Creatives usually express themselves freely amongst each other and refrain from the energy of the non believers. I am here for a Divine Purpose and I need to bring awareness to our creative brothers and sisters of all races, nationalities, ethnicities, that there time is now. That there is a place for them and there always has been and their sister is here to bring awareness and open the dialogue for them and us to reveal themselves boldly, proudly.

It is important for everyone to listen and be in tune with their spirit. Pray for guidance and wisdom. For my empaths, keep shining. Allow the world to glisten with your emotional, intuitive spirit guide. Trust your vibrations and continue to read those energies around you. Continue to protect your energy and trust your Divine instinct.

For those of you that don't know, empaths feel energies, intuition, as in a sixth sense and there are different levels of sensitivity. Empaths are spiritually sensitive and either connect or repel with someone's energy. They are extremely instinctual and can easily either feed off of or become depleted from someone else's energy. If an energy is bad, they will repel it at all costs to instinctually protect their energy. That does not mean that empaths do not make mistakes. But most likely, they ignored an instinct along the way, and trusted or went against what they originally felt or their first mind, and went with pleasure or desire or doubted the original message. This can happen several times and can have a combination of more than one trait.

Seers are known by different names and it all depends on the message, purpose, and spiritual intent. Many of us have had that one family member that always knew when someone was expecting and it was revealed in a dream. They would dream of fish, for example. As I mentioned before, dreams are powerful entities, epiphanies, spiritual messages, warnings, and signs. Can a dream also be a residual of what you watched before bed or something that bothered you and heavily on your mind? Most definitely. Every dream is not necessarily of a deep, spiritual content. However, as stated, I do believe they are of a completely different realm and it is also likely that we do not remember every dream that comes to us. I believe if a message is meant to be revealed, it will move from person to person searching for the person who will reveal its message.

In religion, seers take the name prophet. In other aspects, various names and titles are recognized. In other aspects, it is referred to as priestess in a faith such as Vodoun or Santeria. Sometimes, the name is witch. It's all in our comfortability and your perception of what it is to you. Just like there is good and bad energy, there is the like in purposes. What is the purpose, goal, or intent? Seers do exist and can be a combination of an empath, synesthete or any singular or other combination. Just as anything else, there are different levels. Being in tune with this is nothing in which to be ashamed. In fact, to embrace its reality is to embrace part of your heritage, especially if you are a descendant from a Native American or African bloodline. Society will have you doubting your thoughts and denying the existence of who you are. Simultaneously, movies that have the sixth sense as the subject matter, highlight and monetize these very gifts. The world knows seers exist but they'll have you to believe that to do so is bad. The world will have you to doubt your abilities as coincidence or present it as entertainment or something that you should fear or not discuss. In the end, you cannot deny who or what you are. It is up to you to define that for yourself. Free yourself. Free your mind. Be in tune and pray to The Divine for revelation of your path and blessings along your journey.

Talent, Gifts, And Languages

It is my belief that everyone should speak at least two languages. Our society as a whole is better as a multi lingual, multi communicative society. Many people are resistant to this idea, especially in the United States, which culturally propels the misconception of a multilingual society. This should change. Black Americans, in general, need to make it a priority. Any second or third language is good but since Spanish is the second international language, I recommend Spanish and other languages should follow. And, I do not mean learning basic counting and social phrases, I mean getting deep down into it, and acquiring an in depth knowledge of the language as well as cultural education.

It wasn't until I began traveling that I realized that there are Black people all over the world that speak Spanish: Honduras, Colombia, Panama, Equatorial Guinea Africa, Cuba, Ecuador, Puerto Rico, Mexico, Peru, Bolivia, Costa Rica, Belize, Chile, Trinidad and Tobago and others. Most of us know that there are Blacks that speak Spanish from the Dominican Republic, but unfortunately, many of our brothers and sisters there are unaware that they are Black because they do speak the language. That is sad, but hopefully it can evolve into new knowledge. We speak the language we speak based on our ancestor's colonizer. It's as simple as that. The African blood is still real that courses through our veins and it does not make one subculture greater or more special than the other.

In traveling to Cuba, there is a vast majority of Blacks that look just like Blacks in America but just speak Spanish. Sadly, we are just not aware, in many instances, that each other exists. Growing up, I didn't see that. I only saw the Ricky Ricardo that was placed upon the tv screen and was thrust upon us, giving us a very unrealistic representation and distorted world view. In reality, the minority is the majority when we all come together. We just don't know about each other, and unfortunately it's educationally set up that way. Black people are everywhere and we speak many languages and represent vast cultural entities that link directly to Blacks in America.

It shouldn't be a shock to hear a Black person speaking Spanish. My hope is it gets to the point whereas that is more the norm than the exception. People are not shocked to hear a Black person speaking French, for example, because that is a more common facet of colonization. However, for some reason, the Spanish language, in the minds of some, is reserved for those of a certain skin tone. That's ignorance plain and simple and I am here to dispel that myth. As a Black American who speaks, reads, and writes Spanish, I have experienced racism from those that don't believe that I should know or speak the language, that I shouldn't have access to it. For a time, I allowed that to deter me. Nothing could be further from the truth. No one group of people or subculture holds the right to any one language. Similarly, we as a people need to refrain from rejecting the language and believing the mindset that the language/lenguarse does not pertain to us. The only place that I have been to in America that I have been to thus far where, as a Black person speaking Spanish is a norm rather than an exception is Miami. In Miami, it is more strange if you do not understand la idioma than if you do. I want all people to make more of an effort to embrace it but I especially want Black people to adjust their mindset and think more globally and simultaneously claim what is part of their heritage too. You do not need to be a certain skin color to speak Spanish and until you are able to travel the world and see it and experience it for yourself, trust me and empower yourself by learning to speak, read, and write it immediately. Connect with other Black people that are outside the United States and embrace the many parts of our heritage that you have not explored. Haitian or Jamaican Patwa embrace it and in more than a few phrases than "Yeah Mon". You're capable of much more than that. Refrain from limiting yourself and open your mind fully to the possibilities that exist outside of your immediate world. Find other like minded individuals that connect with your energy.

Explore both your talents and gifts. It is quite possible and probable to possess more than one of each or a combination. As I researched to find the distinction between the two, I found that talents are more skill oriented and gifts are natural, innate abilities regardless of skill level. However, both are extremely important and often intersect with each other. I do believe that a talent is not perfected without the presence of a gift that companions it. Thus, talents and gifts are more a part of each other than not, which makes them almost indiscernible. In essence, talents and gifts go hand in hand and for those of us who grew up in the church, the concepts were often used interchangeably. Thus, the message and key to creativity is to be in tune with your spirit and fully utilize, to the best of your ability, both your talents and gifts. We all have something to offer. Whether it has been discovered or recognized may be an entirely different matter. If you are unaware of what your spiritual gift or talent is, pray about it. Pray that it is revealed and made clear to you. Additionally, if you are wasting your talent(s) or gift(s), cease that practice immediately and change your habits, ways, and thinking. You may be denying someone of the help or guidance that you were created to provide because you are obstinately following your own footsteps and thoughts instead of being spiritually obedient to what is innate.

While I was in high school in Fairfield, California, the organization DLI, Defense Language Institute in Monterey, California tried to recruit me because I had an affinity for languages. I would pick languages up quickly. At that time, I was learning German and eventually changed to Spanish. I also knew some American Sign Language and could imitate most any other language. So much to the point, that people would believe I was speaking an actual language when to me I may have been babbling. Maybe I was speaking a language and I didn't know. The point being, I later realized that I am a natural linguist. I have the gift for languages as well a talent and infinity for such. Even times when I tried to step away from that talent, I was always led back to it.

You need to connect with the right people that can help you develop the skill or your gift and make it a talent. You need a mentor or better yet, mentors.

If you have a child that is always 'babbling' around the house and easily mimics other languages, that may very well be a talent and/or a gift. This may even apply to the very person reading this.

The very things that you dismissed as coincidental, could have very well been signs to lead you to your destiny and purpose. One of my favorite lines in the movie, 'Fools Rush In' is that "there are signs everywhere." Keep that in mind as you explore the direction in which you are propelled in your pursuit of talents, gifts, or languages.

Your talents and gifts can be utilized to uplift others and to make change. In making changes that benefits others can simultaneously benefit you. Give yourself permission to utilize your gifts and talents to propel your economic benefit. I am the last person to tell you to give away what was given to you and to refuse an economic benefit. How you choose to manage your gifts is a personal decision between you and your God. The purpose of my message is for you to be aware, pray for guidance and be in tune with your intuitive messages.

Prayer

I pray that these words resonate with each soul who reads them, but more so to the person and/or persons for whom the message is intended. God, The Divine. Yawah, Jehovah, Jah, Allah, you go by many names and it's not for one person or group to claim you as theirs without the inclusivity of others. I thank you for this opportunity to be your vessel, to be chosen to deliver this message and I pray that I have and continue to be obedient to my spirit. Thank you for all that you've done and you continue to do. Thank you for Favor and Abundant Blessings.

Amen and Ase'

Acknowledgements/ Thank Yous

Thank you to Rev. James H. Brown, for spiritually guiding me through the years. Thank you to my sons, for being my inspiration to persevere...through everything. Thank you to my friends, past and present...you have been a part of my journey and metamorphosis. Thank you to my circle and tribe for always encouraging me and challenging me to be my best.

Thank you to my lion, that makes me smile and my heart smile daily. I am thankful to have you in my life. Ode to the lion and the butterfly.

Thank you to the family that has shown me love throughout the years and has supported me. A special shout out to my Aunt Maxine for listening and being.

I'm grateful for all the church ladies and neighborhood grandmothers growing up.

I'm grateful for meeting the late, great Ntozake Shange. The meeting was divine, for she transitioned six months later. The influence of the late great Toni Morrison, the late, great Zora Neale Hurston, and the late, great Dr. Maya Angelou

Thank you for all the Creatives who continue to break barriers and tear down walls as they sow seeds of hope and purport a higher purpose.

Reflective Thoughts

Reflective Questions

1. What will I do to proactively propel my life towards its future?

___
___
___
___
___
___
___
___
___
___
___
___
___

2. What are five short term goals? What are five long term goals? What is one immediate goal?

3. What is the one take away that I received from this reading?

4. How will I apply what I have learned in 'Butterfliology' Free Thought?

5. What is the new habit I will incorporate into my life?

6. How do others view me as opposed to how I view myself?

7. Thinking back to my earliest childhood memory, what did I want to be and how did I view myself?

_____
_____
_____
_____
_____
_____
_____
_____

8. What is my one positive affirmation I will utilize as my guiding mantra?

_____
_____
_____
_____
_____
_____
_____
_____
_____

9. Which chapter spoke to me the most? Why?

_____
_____
_____
_____
_____
_____
_____
_____
_____

10. What is my new boundary in assuring that I am a Priority?

_____
_____
_____
_____
_____
_____
_____
_____
_____
_____
_____

Johari Window

OPEN SELF

(Known to you and others)

HIDDEN SELF

(Known to you but not known to others)

BLIND SELF

(Known to others but not self)

UNKNOWN SELF

(Not known to you or others)

In reflecting on the Johari Window, there are four selves, or points of view. To work through this exercise, the questions to keep in mind are to discover how you see yourself in relation to how others see you.

1. How do you see yourself? What words would you use to describe yourself?

2. How do others see you? What words would others use to describe me?

_____
_____
_____
_____
_____
_____
_____
_____

3. What do I know about myself that others are not aware? In other words, what is my secret self?

_____
_____
_____
_____
_____
_____
_____
_____

4. What do I not know about myself or have not known about me but am just now discovering? Is there a part of myself that is not known to neither myself or others, and if so, what is that? How do I get to the root core of what that is?

5. Knowing what I know about myself, how do I define myself? Am I more true to my self version or the way others choose to define me?

_____
_____
_____
_____
_____
_____
_____

6. How do I remain true to my authentic self and how do I even know what that is?

_____
_____
_____
_____
_____
_____
_____
_____

7. What steps do I take to refrain from allowing others to define who and what I am?

Resources

'Manifest your Gifts' Dr. Myles Munroe, Steve Harvey, Denzel Washington
https://www.youtube.com/watch?v=vVUFqBcJ68s

'Top Five Legendary Speeches/Motivation for When Life Gets Hard'
https://dailyburstofenergy.com/top-5-legendary-speeches-motivation-for-when-life-gets-hard-goalcast/

'Seeing song through the ears of a synesthete'/Ted Talk®
https://www.youtube.com/watch?v=1LUbxfnpez4

'Seeing Sound: How Synesthesia Can Change Our Thinking'/Annie Dickinson Ted Talk®
https://www.youtube.com/watch?v=88s6guf9egs

'Synesthesia and What it Has Taught Me/Melissa McCracken'/Ted Talk®
https://www.youtube.com/watch?v=kvPd3wH21z8

Resources

Available in major retailers now:

J. Azules Amor's 'Fuego' Erotic Poetry, Passion, and Romance

Contact and Content

For more exclusive content and firsts, subscribe to my patreon.com @ https://www.patreon.com/jamor_azules

www.ingramcontent.com/pod-product-compliance
Lightning Source LLC
Chambersburg PA
CBHW011314080526
44587CB00023B/3996